Teaching the Short Story
Curriculum Guide

with

Reproducible Student Exercises

C. D. Buchanan

American Guidance Service, Inc.
Circle Pines, Minnesota 55014-1796
1-800-328-2560

ISBN 0-7854-0618-2

Product Number 40101

A 0 9 8 7 6 5 4 3 2

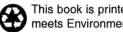 This book is printed on recycled, acid-free paper that
meets Environmental Protection Agency Standards.

Table of Contents

Teaching the Short Story

INTRODUCTION

Clearcut Objectives

Welcome to the wonderful world of the short story! Whether you are an experienced literature teacher, a specialist in some other field, or a generalist with only minimal training in literature instruction, this Guide is for you. Both teacher and student materials are very straightforward and purposeful. The only objectives are 1) to provide your students an enjoyable learning experience as they come to a basic understanding and appreciation of the short story, and 2) to provide you with everything you need to teach a substantive unit on the short story with minimal preparation time.

Why Study the Short Story?

The short story is an ideal vehicle for both teaching and learning. Short stories are a pleasure to present, easy and enjoyable to read, and interesting to discuss. Unlike other forms of great literature, short stories are accessible to virtually every student who can read. As literary forms go, they are not terribly complex or arcane. Most significantly, short stories are *short*—quick to get into and easy to finish.

Everyone loves a good story. The concise action, the limited number of characters, the single plot focus, and the quick resolution are all "friendly factors" that promote both reading competence and confidence. Less able students and more capable students alike will find this introduction to the methods and mechanics of the short story to be an enriching experience.

Stories are a means of transmitting culture. They help us to understand our own history, and they give us insights into human thought and behavior. By opening the door to short stories, you can reveal to your students a path to the world's great legacy of literature and its gifts of personal growth and pleasure. While it is one of the requirements of good fiction to entertain, it is by providing access to the "stuff of life" that literature holds the reader enthralled.

Focus on Concepts and Skills

All the materials in this Guide are concept- and skill-focused. For this reason, the instructional approach is equally appropriate for all students who can read at the fourth grade reading level. Neither the subject matter nor the tone of the student exercises "talk down" to adult students. Middle and junior high students will not be confronted with content matter that is beyond their years. High school students will find the exercises an important reinforcement and enrichment to their basal English program.

Because the teaching plan and the exercises are focused on the *elements of the short story*, this Guide may be used with either adapted versions of short stories or with short stories in their original form. *All* of the students in your class will profit from working on the exercises—no matter what stories they are reading.

FOR TEACHERS OF THE AGS CLASSICS: A SPECIAL NOTE

Great literature is an important part of our human heritage. In the belief that this heritage belongs to everyone, *AGS Classic Short Stories* are adapted to make them accessible to a wide audience of readers who may lack the skill to read them in the original. Lengthy paragraphs and sentences are shortened. Archaic and needlessly difficult words are replaced. Modern punctuation and spellings are used. Many of the longer stories are abridged. In all the stories, painstaking care has been taken to preserve the author's unique voice and style.

A Variety of Authors and Stories

Each book in the *AGS Classic Short Stories* is devoted to the work of a single author. Little-known stories of merit are included with famous old favorites. Taken as a whole, the wealth of authors and stories make up a rich and diverse sampler of the storyteller's art. And AGS Classic Short Stories do more than reflect the personalities, intellects, temperaments, and artistry of their creators. They also illustrate ways in which conditions change with the passing of time. In this way, they communicate a sense of history and provide insight into people's changing responses to changing times.

Appropriate in many Settings

The *AGS Classic Short Stories* are appropriate for such populations as those in Adult Basic Education, prison schools, English as a Second language programs, second track junior high and high school, and self-contained special education classrooms. The stories can be used to upplement a basal language arts program, as an informal survey course, a high-low library resource for pure pleasure reading, an adjunct to social studies instruction, or as a special reading project in any English program.

- *A short introduction* precedes each story. These introductions were designed to arouse the reader's interest and, in many cases, to personalize the story's theme. You may wish to highlight the introductions by reading them aloud or asking a student to read them aloud.

- *A set of discussion questions* is provided for each story at the back of the book. Use these as you wish. Since all questions focus on the elements of the short story, you may want to assign them as homework, for extra credit activities, or for discussion in small study groups.

- *A scene-setting illustration* introduces each story. When possible, discuss the artwork with the students. As a pre-reading activity, ask students what information the illustration provides about the characters, setting, mood, or events in the story. Point out that each drawing and its caption communicate through a combination of words and graphics, just as today's newspapers and magazines do.

- *A brief author biography* appears at the beginning of each book. These biographies present the authors as hard-working, flesh and blood people rather than as literary icons. The biographies are an important resource to the students' understanding of the stories. They help students to place both the author and his or her work in time. The biographies also show how the author's interests and experiences helped to shape the stories.

- *A booklet of Teacher's Notes* is provided with each set of ten books, e.g. *Great American Short Stories I*. The information in the *Notes* will prove extremely useful in tailoring your instruction to the exact needs of your students. Each booklet of *Notes* contains the following material for every story: a capsule summary of setting and story plot, three or four focal points you might use to teach the story, a list of the proper names in the story, a key vocabulary list, and a list of the idiomatic expressions used in the story.

By quickly scanning this material before presenting a story, you can easily identify the words and phrases that may prove challenging to your particular students. As a pre-reading activity, you may want to list some of the words on the chalkboard and discuss their meanings before students meet the words in context. Idiomatic expressions may be an especially useful area of study for ESL students, for example. But the importance of this extracted information for practice in spelling, pronunciation, and general vocabulary-building should not be overlooked for all your students.

A BRIEF HISTORY OF THE SHORT STORY

The Spoken Story

Of all the arts, storytelling is surely the oldest. Long before the dawn of history, primitive peoples must have found delight in talking about their success in the hunt or their cunning in the fight. No doubt the storyteller's imagination soon taught him when to drop superfluous facts and when to add details in order to improve their stories. In the course of time, these simple narratives of personal adventure were combined with attempts to explain the powerful forces of nature, thereby helping to create the myth, the hero-tale, the legend, and the folktale.

These early stories were undoubtedly crude and formless at first. But they were eventually given some sort of shape by the professional storyteller who seems to have been common to all peoples and all literatures at some early stage in their development. And of course, as these stories were told and retold, they were added to, remolded, and thus handed down orally from one generation to another.

The Written Story

All around the world, human cultures have produced their tales, legends, fables, sketches, parables, and anecdotes. The great story-telling poems of Homer, preserved in written form, are products of ancient Greece, as are Aesop's fables. The Bible contains many examples of short stories. Geoffery Chaucer's *Canterbury Tales*, from the 14th century, contain short story forms. But while there is a long tradition of storytelling in the history of literature, the short story form as we know it today is less than 200 years old.

The Modern Short Story

The modern short story, with its formal characteristics of length, focus, and style, developed as an art form in the 19th century. Washington Irving (1783-1859), famous for his picturesque sketches and moral tales, was the first of the great American short story writers.

Nathaniel Hawthorne (1804-1864) and Edgar Allan Poe (1809-1849) both made enormous contributions to the development and definition of the short story form. Poe carefully refined the "single effect," for which the short story is now known. Hawthorne brought a focus on the psychological development of characters.

The middle and latter years of the 19th century saw the short story take hold in other parts of the world as well. Flaubert and Maupassant in France, and the great Russian writers Tolstoy, Dostoevsky, and Chekhov, just to name a few, contributed greatly to the short story's acceptance worldwide.

As the short story grew in popularity, magazines rushed to publish the growing number of new writers. At the same time, of course, the world itself was changing. Education was becoming almost common property, and reading was becoming a universal habit. But as the world became more complicated, so did the lives of ordinary people. Leisure time for reading diminished as the pace of life picked up. By the turn of the century, a hundred readers could find time for a short story to every one reader who could devote him or herself to a long novel.

The short story, therefore, filled a natural want created in large part by the conditions of modern life. In America, the Golden Era of the short story paralleled the Golden Era of the magazine. Both began to decline when television became the popular new medium of communication and entertainment about 1950. Today, however, the form and style of the short story continue to evolve in the hands of many gifted writers.

PRESENTING THE SHORT STORY

Warm-up

Before presenting any one short story, be sure to remind your students that fiction is a form of communication as well as an art form. Tell them that fiction reflects life—distilled through the author's sensibilities and experience. Point out to your students that short stories represent links in the chain of human experience. Stories connect readers with men and women who have attempted to say something about life through their art.

And, of course, these writers who lived in different times and in different places have different stories to tell.

Since each writer speaks in his or her own unique voice, the stories exhibit a wide range of differences. They are of various types, they treat various themes, and they use various stylistic devices. At the same time, all stories exhibit certain similarities. All use language to express ideas; they address common life experiences; and they involve people, thoughts, places, action, and time. They all use the modern short story form.

In gaining understanding of the points of similarity and difference among many stories, your students will add to their understanding and enjoyment of literature, of life, and of themselves.

ANALYZING A SHORT STORY

TITLE

Tell students that the title of a short story may serve various purposes. Following is a list of the most common:

- To give the name of the principal character, as in "Tony Kytes, the Arch-Deceiver" (Hardy)
- To give the theme or setting of the story, as in "Quality" (Galsworthy)
- To suggest the chief incident, as in "An Occurrence at Owl Creek Bridge" (Bierce)
- To name some object which plays an important part in the story, as in "The Skeleton" (Tagore)
- To suggest the type of the story, as in "The Mysterious Mansion" (Balzac)
- To give the tone of the story, as in "The Specter" (Maupassant)
- To arouse curiosity, as in "The Lady or the Tiger?" (Stockton)

Ask your students to identify which of these purposes the story title serves. Does it seem to have a purpose that is not mentioned in the above list? Ask students to give their opinions as to whether the title is well chosen.

BEGINNING

Point out that the opening paragraphs of a story may also serve various purposes. Following is a list of the most common:

- To launch the action of the story, either with an incident or a conversation
- To introduce characters, by description or comment
- To give the setting by describing the scene of the story
- To state or hint at the main idea of the story
- To tell how the story came to be told or written

Ask your students to decide what purpose or purposes are served by the first paragraph or two of the story. Do they serve any purpose not mentioned above? Did the beginning of the story make them want to read on?

PLOT

Explain that the basic definition of plot is "what happens to the characters." Point out that one way to classify plots is on the basis of their p*robability*. The three groupings in this plan are *probable*, *improbable*, and *impossible*. Use the paradigm that in realistic fiction the plot is always probable, in romantic fiction it may well be improbable, and in science fiction, impossible. Some of the following questions about plot will prove useful:

- Is the plot of this story probable, improbable, or impossible?
- What is the pace (movement) of the story? Do events come one after another quickly, gradually, or slowly?

- Is the story interesting throughout? Is there any point where the reader's interest flags?

CLIMAX

Interest is at its highest pitch at the climax of the story. In many stories, the whole plot is built around the climax—the story exists for this, and when the climax is reached, the story ends. In other stories, such as the old-fashioned tale, the climax is less important.

- * What is the climax of the story? Does the whole story rest on the outcome or climax?
- * Are there minor climaxes in the story? Where?
- * Are there one or more incidents in the story that help plot development? What were those incidents? How did they help the plot keep moving?

CHARACTERS

Vivid characterization is essential to effective storytelling. Explain that there are four ways of showing character: 1) by the author's comment; 2) by the comment of other characters; 3) by what a character does; and 4) by what a character says.

- Which of the four methods listed above does the author use to reveal his or her characters? Ask students to give an example.
- Does the author tend to use one method more than the others?
- To what social class do the characters belong? Why is that important?
- Are there many or few characters in the story?
- Are the characters lifelike? Give an example. Do they seem artificial or false in any way? Give an example.
- Did the author give a physical description of the characters? If not, what do your

students imagine that the characters looked like?

SETTING

The time and place of a story may be directly stated, hinted at, or in some cases, not mentioned at all. Explain that setting gives important clues about the nature of a story. Time and place are the "mental backdrop" of the stage on which the story will play out. The characters and events can best be understood if setting is well established in the reader's mind.

- Are the surroundings made clear? Does the author give the detailed appearance of a village street, the interior of a house, etc.? If so, why?

- Is there much description of nature? Is it important to the story?

- Is the setting purposely shadowy or vague? Did the author do this to create a certain atmosphere or tone in the scene?

- Is there much use of local color? What aspects of the setting could only have been used to describe that particular time and place and no other?

STYLE

Introduce the concept of "writer's style" by suggesting that there are styles of written expression just as there are styles in any other area of personal expression. To help your students understand written style, have them think about *spoken* styles—the characteristic ways in which different people talk. For example, some people speak gruffly, some are always joking, and some speak in flowery or very formal language. Help your students understand that style reveals personality and that it involves not only the words used, but the way in which the words are used.

- Which of the following words might describe the style of the story: *graphic and startling, easy and flowing, riveting, intense, careful* and *controlled, polished, wordy, flat, sarcastic, gentle*? Encourage students to come up with their own terms of description.

- Is the story told chiefly through narration or through conversation?

- Is the style clear?

- Is the author's personality revealed by his or her style? How?

- How does the author use unfamiliar or technical terms? Are these terms defined in the story? Can you guess what they mean from their context in the sentence or paragraph?

- Does the author use many figures of speech? Have students point out some figures of speech. Discuss what is gained by their use.

- Does the author's style have individuality? After reading several of his or her stories, could a reader recognize the author's work?

PRESENTING THE EXERCISES

Part II of this Guide, *Studying the Short Story*, consists of 40 reproducible exercises. The format of these exercises provides a structure for analyzing and studying any and all stories. Be sure to present the exercises as aids to learning and understanding, rather than as tests or tedious chores. Explain that the point of the activities is not necessarily to "get all the right answers," but to stimulate and guide thinking in a creative but structured way. Note that each section of exercises contains at least one "advanced" activity. In general, these are writing exercises that will challenge your best students.

Organization

It is a good plan to set up a folder for each student. Either you or the student can file and keep all the completed exercises there. Your more interested and able students may complete all of the exercises for each story read. Others may pick and choose, completing at least one exercise from each section for every story read. At minimum, it is recommended that every student should complete the following exercises for each book read: *Story Report*, *Time Line*, and *Vocabulary*.

One way to handle all the paper is to begin ahead of time by making sufficient copies of all the exercises for your class. You might place them between labeled dividers in a file drawer or a box. Then you can give students free access to the exercises or distribute them yourself. A reproducible master list of exercises is provided in Section VII. Students may use their copy of this record sheet to check off all the exercises they have completed. For handy reference, all students should have a copy of the glossary and time lines for their folders.

The exercises are divided into seven sections.

Section I: THE ART OF FICTION

- Categories of Art (Discussion Starter)
- The Writer's Tools (Concept Setter)
- Story Elements (Discussion Starter)
- The Form of the Short Story (Concept Setter)
- Types of Stories
- Artful Language (Concept Setter)
- Artful Language (Advanced)

These activities are designed for presentation in a discussion setting. They are intended to provoke and develop thought, and to encourage students to be at ease with art. The exercises themselves are self-explanatory. *Your* enthusiasm for the topics—and your willingness to expand on them with examples from your own experience—will greatly enhance their effectiveness. If you cannot present these activities in a discussion setting, assign them for independent completion. Try to follow up with discussion.

Discussion points: Explain to your students that every culture expresses itself through art. According to the dictionary, art is "the human ability to make things; the creativity of people as distinguished from the world of nature." Help your students to become aware of the art that is around us, all the time. Whether we think about it or not, our lives are affected by the design of the buildings we live in, the music we hear, the color and shape of the clothes we wear, and so on.

Introduce the idea of fiction as a form of art—a unique human expression of the life experience. In every way that you can, disabuse your students of the notion that art is pretentious, snobbish, or the sophisticated domain of only the wealthy and well-educated. Point out that Navajo rugs are art, jazz music is art, as is the design of a bus or the pattern on wallpaper. Tell your students that short stories are artworks made by writers. Like all art, a main purpose of short stories is to communicate. Every writer has something to say that he or she wants other people to understand.

Section II: SETTING

- Defining Setting
- Analyzing Setting
- Setting and Time
- Settings in Your Life

- Writing About Setting
- Story Report: Setting

Discussion points: The events of every story obviously happen at a certain place and time. Together, the place and time make up the story's setting. (Refer students to their glossary handout.) Time is frequently very important to setting. For example, a setting such as New York City will differ from one century to the next. The time depicted—past, present, or future—will affect the nature of the setting. You will want to point out that time of year and even time of day may be crucial to understanding a story's unfolding events.

Explain that it is important for a reader to rather quickly determine where and when the story is taking place. This is how readers form a mental context for the action. Your students may find it useful to pretend that the story they are reading is a movie they are directing. Where will it be filmed? What will the characters be wearing? What will their surroundings look like? What important events (a war, storm, drought, fatal illness) are taking place? What thoughts will be dominating the characters' minds? Bring the concept of setting to life by explaining that the writer is like a painter, set designer, and historian, all in one. To be convincing, the picture that the writer paints must be true to life.

Section III: PLOT

- Defining Plot
- Analyzing Plot: Conflict and Resolution
- Story Structure
- Plots in Your Life
- Writing About Plot
- Story Report: Plot

Discussion points: Plot can quickly be defined as "what happens in a story." (Refer students to their glossary handout.) Tell your students that a story isn't a story if nothing happens. A good plot usually involves a conflict or a struggle of some kind, followed by a resolution. The struggle may be internal ("Should I do it?") or external ("That man is pointing a gun at *me*!").

If the plot of a short story is too complex, it may be confusing. If it's too simplistic, the story may be boring. A well-crafted plot is the key to a great story. A story with a strong plot may often succeed in spite of weaknesses such as uninteresting characters or an ill-defined setting. Without an effective plot, a story will not hold a reader's interest.

Some plots are based on action, some on suspense, some on a clash between characters, and some on internal conflicts. Plots vary widely. But in the best short stories, everything that happens contributes in some way to the conflict and its resolution. Help your students to become good "plot detectives." Encourage them to look for the relationship of every event to the unfolding plot. Does the plot contain a surprising twist? Many of the world's best-loved stories are built around this popular literary device.

Section IV: CHARACTER

- Defining Character
- Analyzing Character
- Understanding Characters
- Characters in Your Life
- Writing About Character
- Story Report: Character

Discussion points: There is no story without characters. (Refer students to their glossary handout.) The characters may be people, animals, ghosts, or sometimes even inanimate objects. The "who or what" that figure into the story's action and struggle are its characters. Using very few words, the writer must bring the story's characters to life. How do writers make us care about their characters, see them in our minds, like or dislike them, understand them? Encourage your students to play close attention to the characters in each story: What facts are revealed about them? Often, appreciating the characters is the key to getting the most out of the story. What intelligent guesses can the reader make about them? What clues has the author provided? How are the characters alike and different? What characters are most important to the story? What important clues to the characters are expressed in dialogue? In action? In description? How clearly are the characters drawn? Do your students feel they "know" the characters? Does one character stand out in the story? In the reader's mind? Do the characters change in the course of the story?

Section V: THEME

- Defining Theme
- Analyzing Theme
- Writing About Theme
- Story Report: Theme

Discussion points: Every story has a theme, but discovering a story's theme is not a cut-and-dried matter. (Refer students to their glossary handout.) Discussing themes can be one of the most interesting aspects of studying the short story. Encourage your students to think in terms of the categories of great literary themes: love, death, life-struggle, jealousy, greed, revenge—the whole range of human emotions.

While a story might neatly fit into a category—such as war—the author's message may not be so neatly revealed. Always discuss the themes of the stories your students read. Train your students to look for the underlying, universal theme before they look for the author's individual message. Sometimes a main character will state the author's message. Sometimes the story's main point will be subtly expressed by a supporting character, or by a remark made by the narrator. Accept a variety of interpretations of the story's theme. Like all works of art, stories will say different things to different people.

Section VI: TONE AND MOOD

- Defining Tone
- Defining Mood
- Analyzing Mood
- Writing About Mood
- Story Report: Mood

Discussion points: Tone and mood are less important elements of fiction than plot, setting, character, and theme. But tone and mood are significant to the *effect* of a story. Literary methods of creating feeling are quite varied among writers. Some writers, such as Poe, become distinctive stylists in conveying dark and dramatic moods. Some, like Mark Twain, set a humorous tone. Identifying the tone and mood of a story is often a subjective matter. Encourage your students to be sensitive to these artistic devices. Call their attention to the author's use of language in creating a given effect. Have students look for descriptions and characterizations that build suspense, create apprehension or expectation, and otherwise manipulate the reader's emotions. Encourage students to apply these devices to their own writing.

Section VII: ADDITIONAL RESOURCES

The following materials are provided for your students.

- Glossary Handout
- Generic Vocabulary Exercise
- Generic Story Report
- Generic Story Report, Advanced
- Generic Time Line Exercises: United States and World
- Student Record Sheet: Stories
- Student Record Sheet: Exercises

Using the Additional Resources

The Glossary and Time Lines should be reproduced for all students and placed in their folders. The Vocabulary and Story Report exercises in Section VII are generic—they can be used again and again with each story. The Student Record sheets enable students to track their own progress. Use of the Vocabulary exercises is especially important in encouraging your students' language development. All the resources in this section will help your students build good study habits such as frequent use of a dictionary, cross-referencing information, and note-taking.

Using the Time Line Exercises

Placing a piece of literature in historic context is an important aid to understanding. If students are to understand why an author wrote a certain type of story or focused on certain events, they must first have some grasp of the times in which the story was written. Did the author write in a time of war? A time of great discovery? Had the automobile been invented? The electric light? What were living conditions like? Political conditions? What were people's hopes and dreams in that particular time and place?

The two generic time line exercises can help students get a clearer picture of the times that produced the writer who produced the stories. One time line is provided for placing American stories, and one is for placing stories from other parts of the world. The left side of each time line exercise lists key historical events in chronological order. The right side of each time line has blank spaces for the students to fill in.

A time line is a wonderful discussion-starter. You may want your students to record the birth and death dates of various authors or the date a story was first published. This activity could set up a discussion on the relationship between technology and art or politics and art. You might want students to place story characters in time and then discuss why certain characters could not have been created earlier (a Gold Rush prospector, for example, could not have appeared before the Gold Rush). The uses of these time lines will be limited only by your imagination.

Focusing on Vocabulary

The work of vocabulary building is crucial in all fields of learning. For this reason, it is important to copy a sufficient supply of vocabulary exercises so that all of your students can use them with every story. Short stories provide an ideal framework for vocabulary work. Rather than trying to learn unfamiliar words in isolation, your students will find it much easier to make educated guesses about difficult words when they come across them in context.

Before you assign the vocabulary exercises, emphasize to your students that literature is a *form of communication*. The words an author uses, and the way in which they are used, are essential to the author's message—just as the fund of words the student has to draw on will form and shape his or her own expression of thought and experience. Point out that it is in the student's own interest to make frequent additions to his or her own word bank.

Using the Glossary

The glossary of literary terms provided is intended to familiarize your students with the basic vocabulary necessary to any serious discussion of literature. You will find it worth your time to help your students become comfortable in using these terms by planning several mini-lessons around the glossary.

A simple extension of the information provided in the glossary is to assign your students to write their own "example sentences" to illustrate each term. A challenge exercise might be to have students create small crossword puzzles with six or more terms. In this activity, students might work in pairs, one arranging the graphics and one writing the clues.

After reading any story, your students might be assigned to select any four or five words from the glossary, list them on a piece of paper, and then find examples in the story to demonstrate their understanding of each term's definition.

As with all vocabulary work, regular use of the new words in context promotes retention and mastery.

Putting it All Together

Beyond simple reading practice, the primary purpose of assigning short stories to your students is to encourage their interest in literature as a whole. This is best accomplished by providing access to interesting, stimulating material, and then facilitating the assimilation of the material through discussion and other extension activities.

The exercises provide an organized approach to analysis of the story material, as well as many opportunities for lively discussion. Clearly, this structured practice with the elements of fiction will enhance their reading far beyond their present assignment. To further extend the learning experience, encourage your students to write as often as possible. By directly participating in the creative process themselves, they will inevitably become more discerning, appreciative readers.

Answer Key—Student Exercises

Exercise 1: 1. architecture; 2. film; 3. sculpture; 4. fiction; 5. drama; 6. dance; 7. music; 8. music, theater; 9. nonfiction; 10. theater; 11. painting, photography; 12. theater, film; 13. nonfiction; 14. poetry.

Exercise 2: 1. description; 2. dialogue; 3. narrative; 4. balanced.

Exercise 3: Characters—firefighter, sports hero, thief, father; Dialogue—insults, questions, explanations, statements, jokes; Plot—secrets, actions, adventure, surprises; Setting—farm, long ago, present, city, future, outer space; Feelings—anger, fear, sorrow, love, excitement.

Exercise 4: (Part I) 2, 4, 1, 3; (Part II) 5. an animal; 6. She has a bad memory. She forgot where it was. 7. middle; 8. happy.

Exercise 5: 1. "Ten Days on a Life Raft" 2. "The Day We Met the Martians" 3. "A Treasure Hunt in the Jungle" 4. "Rosalie's Romance" 5. "The Detective's Strangest Case" 6. "The Return of the Undead" 7. mystery, adventure; 8. horror, sea; 9. love, adventure; 10. mystery, science fiction.

Exercise 6: 1. c; 2. b; 3. a; 4. b; 5. c; 6. c.

Exercise 7: 1. scary; 2. calm; 3. delicious; 4. conflict; 5. joy; 6. hateful; 7. cold; 8. inviting; 9. sorrow; 10. hot.

Exercise 8: Setting: where and when a story takes place; the location and the time; 1. c, more description of place and time than in other paragraphs; 2. b, c; 3. c; 4. c; 5. a; 6. Answers will vary.

Exercise 9: 1. mountain cabin; 2. city park; 3. wagon train; 4. restaurant; 5. school; 6. spaceship; 7. bus.

Exercise 10: 1. can't tell; 2. past; 3. past; 4. present; 5. past; 6. can't tell; 7. past; 8. present.

Exercises 11-13: Answers will vary.

Exercise 14: Plot: the chain of events in a story that leads to its outcome; 1. b; 2. The fawn has been left an orphan. It's mother has been killed. 3. no, too many horses for the grasslands to feed, overbreeding, etc. 4. The boys raise the fawn. 5. Answers will vary.

Exercise 15: 1. the outcome of the story's main conflict; 2. (underline) After 20 minutes of dodging and wheeling on his horse, he gave up. (problem) The lieutenant felt uncomfortable about being followed by a wolf. 3. (underline) This gifted woman taught Helen to communicate—first by touch and then with speech. (problem) Helen was deaf and blind. She couldn't communicate. 4. (underline) Then they both began to laugh. (problem) Gary and Maryann didn't want their parents to marry. 5. (underline) "Surprise!" everybody yelled, as he bolted through the front door. (problem) Harlan is late getting home to celebrate his birthday. He's not prepared for the celebration.

Exercise 16: (page 1) 1. Alex and Ben Johnson; 2. a; 3. Alex's painting wins first place. 4. Answers will vary. (page 2) 1. Alex asks Ben to deliver a painting to the museum. 2. Ben spills shellac on the painting. He wraps up the painting in brown paper. 3. Ben is horrified to see that bits of wrapping paper are stuck to the painting. He runs off. 4. Ben sleeps poorly and has bad dreams. 5. Ben decides to either get help fixing the painting or tell Alex about the accident. 6. Ben can't find Alex's painting. 7. Ben sees that Alex's painting has won first prize. 8. three; 9. Ben's accident with the shellac ruined the painting. 10. seven; 11. Ben; 12. four; 13. Answers will vary.

Exercises 17-19: Answers will vary.

Exercise 20: 1. a fictional person who plays a part in a story; 2. e; 3. and 4. Answers will vary.

Exercise 21: 1. a.description, b.dialogue, c.dialogue, d.narration; 2. a, c, e, g, h; 3. j, k, m, p; 4. Answers will vary.

Exercise 22: 1. no; 2. Marty; 3. frightening; Answers will vary. 4. Marty; 5. danger, gloom; 6. Marty, no; 7. Howard. He likes bright lights and familiar sounds around him.

Exercises 23-25: Answers will vary.

Exercise 26: Theme: the central meaning of a story; the main idea; the point; 1.-12. Answers will vary.

Exercise 27: 1. love, disappointment; 2. sacrifice, honor, war; 3. art, success, sacrifice; 4. art, courage; 5. sacrifice, love; 6. family, love; 7. kindness, courage; 8. courage, disappointment; 9. family, misunderstanding; 10. disappointment; 11. injustice, greed; 12. hope, courage.

Exercises 28-29: Answers will vary.

Exercise 30: 1. the feeling given by the author's voice; the attitude expressed by the author's use of language; 2. mysterious; 3. humorous; 4. confiding; 5. suspicious; 6. hopeless; 7. sarcastic; 8. frightening.

Exercise 31: Mood: the overall feeling or atmosphere the author creates in a story; 1. gloomy; 2. Answers will vary; 3. scary; 4. fearful.

Exercise 32: 1. sadness; 2. joy; 3. excitment; 4. loneliness; 5. despair; 6. fear.

Exercises 33-34: Answers will vary.

THE ART OF FICTION: Categories of Art

Name _____ Date _____

What does the word *art* mean to you? Does it make you think of painting or dancing on a stage or writing a play? Art is all of those things and more. Art is the human creation of something that has form and beauty. Art is the expression and communication of a person's ideas and experiences. Making art is one of the main activities of being a human being.

Art is divided into broad categories. Within each category, there are many forms. The chart below shows some of the categories of the fine arts and the forms within them.

Visual Arts	Performing Arts	Literary Arts
painting	music	fiction
photography	dance	nonfiction
sculpture	theater	drama
architecture	film	poetry

Each category of art contains many forms. For example, fiction is a form of the literary arts, and the short story is a form of fiction. Read the list of examples below. Next to each example, write its form. Choose a word from the box. You may use a word more than once.

1. a church _____

2. a movie _____

3. a statue _____

4. a novel _____

5. a play _____

6. a ballet _____

7. a jazz band _____

8. an opera _____

9. a book review _____

10. a magic show _____

11. a portrait _____

12. acting _____

13. a dictionary _____

14. a sonnet _____

Teaching the Short Story Curriculum Guide © 1994 Lake Education, Belmont CA

THE ART OF FICTION: The Writer's Tools

Name _____   Date _____

Narration is the telling of the story, or recital of events.

Example: Alice was late. She dressed in a hurry and raced out the door. She had to run to the bus stop. Then she realized that she had left her lunch at home.

Description is the language that tells you how something or someone looks or feels.

Example: Alice was late. Her shoes were untied and her coat was buttoned up wrong. She sprinted toward the bus stop, out of breath from running.

Dialogue is words spoken or thought by characters in the story.

Example: "Wait!" Alice cried, running down the walk. "Please tell the driver to wait!" "I overslept," Alice told the driver. "I've had no breakfast, and I forgot my lunch!"

**Label each paragraph below *narration, description,* or *dialogue.*
One paragraph is a balance of all three tools. Label that paragraph
balanced. (Hint: Read all the paragraphs first.)**

1. The sun shone with a white-hot intensity. Two sunburned men
    struggled across the barren desert. One kept falling, and the other
    helped him up. Both men were in rags. They both felt terrible thirst.
    A large cactus cast its shadow about 30 feet away.

    _____

2. "Come on, Joe, you can make it!" Al pulled his brother to his feet.
    "The sun's so hot," whispered Joe. "The sky seems to be burning."
    "Here, lean on me. Just a few more steps, now," Al urged.
    "I'm so thirsy," Joe gasped, through dry lips. "I don't want to move."
    "Put one foot in front of the other," Al said. "That cactus may hold water."

    _____

3. The sun shone with a white-hot intensity. To Joe the blue sky seemed
    to be burning. He put one foot in front of the other, trying to keep up
    with his brother. It took all his strength just to take one step. Then he
    fell. Al picked him up. He fell again. Again Al picked him up. In this
    stumbling way, the two men moved on. Each painful step brought
    them closer to the cactus and its little patch of shade.

    _____

4. The sun blazed down as the two brothers struggled across the barren
    desert. Joe fell again. "Come on, little brother," urged Al, pulling Joe to
    his feet. "You can make it." Joe did as his brother said. He put one foot
    in front of the other. Maybe there was water in that big cactus ahead.

    _____

THE ART OF FICTION: Story Elements

Name _____ Date _____

A writer uses building blocks to create a story. These building blocks are called the *elements of fiction*. Each heading in the following chart is one of the elements of fiction.

Below the chart is a list of subjects that a writer might use in a story. Place each subject under the correct heading. Some subjects may go in more than one category. Use your glossary if you need help with the headings.

ELEMENTS OF FICTION				
Characters	Dialogue	Plot	Setting	Feelings

Subjects

a firefighter	fear	secrets	surprises
anger	jokes	outer space	love
a farm	a city	adventure	sorrow
long ago	insults	a thief	explanations
the present	the future	statements	a father
a sports hero	questions	actions	excitement

THE ART OF FICTION: The Form of the Short Story

Name _____ Date _____

Part I   **Every story has a beginning, a middle, and an end. Read the paragraphs below. When they are put in order, the paragraphs make a short story. Show their correct order by numbering the paragraphs.**

_____   Time passed, and the acorn sprouted into a seedling. It put roots down into the earth. It put a slender stem up toward the light. In the warm spring sun, the seedling grew tall.

_____   One spring, the old oak was blown down in a storm. Its rotting trunk became the home for many new animals. Nearby several new seedlings were growing. One was nearly six feet tall. They had all grown from acorns buried by absent-minded squirrels.

_____   In the beginning, an acorn was buried in the earth by a squirrel. The squirrel had a bad memory and a large family to feed. In the hurly burly of squirrel life, she forgot where she had buried the acorn.

_____   After many years, the oak tree towered among the other trees in the park. Many squirrels had nests in its branches. But, sadly, some of its branches were rotting. The oak had become diseased. It was growing too weak to stand.

Part II   **Now answer the following questions about the story.**

5. Is the main character in this story an animal or a person?

_____

6. Why doesn't she dig up the acorn to feed her family? _____

_____

7. Is the first seedling mentioned in the middle of the story or the end?

_____

8. Does this story have a sad ending or a happy ending? _____

_____

Teaching the Short Story Curriculum Guide © 1994 Lake Education, Belmont CA

THE ART OF FICTION: Types of Stories

Name _____ Date _____

Part I   There are many different kinds of stories. Often, the story's title hints at what kind of story it is. Read the story types on the left and the titles on the right. Then draw a line to match each title with its category.

1.	sea story	"A Treasure Hunt in the Jungle"
2.	science fiction story	"Ten Days on a Life Raft"
3.	adventure story	"The Day We Met the Martians"
4.	love story	"Rosalie's Romance"
5.	mystery story	"The Return of the Undead"
6.	horror story	"The Detective's Strangest Case"

Part II   Some stories belong to two or more types. A sea story, for example, may also be an adventure story. Each sentence below describes a story that belongs to two categories. After each sentence, write two of the story types listed above.

7.   A private investigator solves a crime by sneaking into a criminal's mountaintop hideaway. _____ and

_____

8.   The ghost of a murdered sailor returns to haunt his shipmates.

_____ and _____

9.   A man risks his life to find his sweetheart in a blinding snowstorm.

_____ and _____

10.   A robot comes to life and steals government secrets. The FBI puts 100 agents on the case. _____ and

_____

THE ART OF FICTION: Artful Language

Name _____ Date _____

A writer's artful use of language can tell us a lot in just a few words. Read the short paragraph below. Then circle a letter to answer each question.

> Ramon was afraid of dogs. But when he saw the little poodle trembling on the ice, he knew he had to help. The puppy was not very far from the shore, but it was afraid to move. Whining and shivering on the frozen pond, the poodle was a pitiful sight.

1. How does the writer let us know that Ramon is a kind person?

   a. She says that Ramon is kind.

   b. She tells about Ramon's many friends.

   c. She says that Ramon wants to help the dog.

2. What words make us feel sympathy for the poodle?

   a. pond, ice, far

   b. little, pitiful, trembling

   c. dog, shore, move

3. How does the writer hint that something will happen?

   a. She presents a problem to solve.

   b. She writes about dogs.

   c. She describes Ramon's looks.

4. What has the writer accomplished in this paragraph?

   a. She has presented a problem and its solution.

   b. She has made us wonder how the problem will be solved.

   c. She has explained how the dog got there.

5. What word describes the sound the puppy was making?

   a. shivering

   b. trembling

   c. whining

6. What words tell us that it is winter?

   a. afraid of dogs

   b. shore, pitiful

   c. frozen, ice

THE ART OF FICTION: Artful Language, Advanced

Name _____ Date _____

Writers use language to create different effects. Their words can make us see things, feel things, and even taste things. Read the sentences. Use a word from the box to label the effect created by each sentence.

EFFECTS						
calm	scary	delicious	pain	cold	hot	inviting
conflict	joy	sorrow	hateful	kind	suspenseful	gloomy

1. The snarling lion flashed his teeth and jumped at Pam. _____

2. Fields of corn stretched as far as the eye could see under a cloudless blue sky. _____

3. The sizzling chicken was wrapped in a cloud of fragrant steam. _____

4. "No, you don't," yelled Jon, pushing the bully away. But the bigger boy was much stronger, and he knocked Jon to the ground. _____

5. It was the most beautiful face Carol had ever seen, and it belonged to her father. "Oh, Dad, I've missed you so much," Carol cried, running into his arms. _____

6. The man kicked the puppy again and again. The more it cried, the harder he kicked. _____

7. The winter sky was so black the snow looked gray. Stars blazed overhead like tiny points of frozen light. _____

8. A bright fire crackled in the fireplace. Two comfortable chairs stood beside a table that held a steaming pot of tea. "Come in," smiled Aunt Nell. _____

9. Tonya knew her mother would not get well. She stood beside the bed with tears rolling down her cheeks. _____

10. The sun beat down on the white sand. Nothing stirred on the scorching beach. _____

SETTING: Defining Setting

Name _____ Date _____

Look up the term *setting* in your glossary. Write the definition here.

_____

_____

Now think about setting as you read the three paragraphs below. Then answer the questions.

a.   Catherine had no desire to be out on the snowy streets. In winter, she always spent more time practicing the piano. Her music teacher was pleased with her progress. When the weather warmed up, however, it was a different story.

b.   John was up before dawn to do his farm chores. But the afternoons were his. Then he drove high into the hills, where the trails were packed with snow. He was the fastest skier on his school's team.

c.   The evening star shone in the sky. Dave led his pony to the lake to drink. The golden moon was reflected in the water. Dave looked out on the vast prairie, shimmering in the moonlight. He had never seen anything so beautiful.

1.   Which paragraph gives the best description of setting? _____

Explain your decision. _____

_____

_____

2.   Which two paragraphs are set in the country? _____ and _____

3.   Which paragraph is set at night? _____

4.   Which paragraph is *not* set in winter? _____

5.   Which paragraph has an indoor setting? _____

6.   Which setting is most appealing to you? Why? _____

_____

_____

_____

SETTING: Analyzing Setting

Name _____ Date _____

At the end of each paragraph, name the setting it describes. Choose from the words in the box.

spaceship	mountain cabin	city park	restaurant	bus	school	wagon train

1. The sound of the wind woke me. Branches scraped at the roof, and the rustling of the leaves was almost a roar. This would be a bad storm. The banging sound I heard must be a loose shutter. Groping in the dark, I found a match and lit the lantern.

   _____

2. My grandfather had a favorite bench where we would sit on summer afternoons. There was so much to see! Mothers pushed baby carriages. Horseback riders cantered down the shady paths. Sometimes we fed the birds.

   _____

3. Day after day, the oxen plodded on. Ten mounted men rode ahead of the party, and three brought up the rear. There wasn't much to see— just miles of flat prairie grasses, with a twisted tree here and there.

   _____

4. Gary was very nervous. It was his first day. He was to bring water to the tables as soon as people sat down. He was to remove plates at just the right time. It didn't seem too hard. But what if he spilled water on someone?

   _____

5. Only a few more minutes were left. Alice was worried. What if Mr. Nelson called on her? She hadn't read the lesson! Alice glanced at her watch. Only one more minute. And then, oh, no! "Alice Korvallis, can you explain the reasons for the fall of Rome?" Alice hoped the bell would ring.

   _____

6. There wasn't one inch of extra space on the ship. Each crew member had a bunk, but every other nook and cranny was community property. Everyone was always glad to reach the end of a long voyage. To be able to walk around outside after long months in orbit was be a great luxury.

   _____

7. There was no place to sit, but Ken was glad to be on board. He braced himself as they lurched to a stop and jerked forward again. It was so crowded that the riders bumped shoulders all the way to midtown. There several people got off. Ken sank happily into an empty seat.

   _____

SETTING: Setting and Time

Name _____ Date _____

Time is important to setting. The story of your life might mention television, jet travel, and computers. But those things were not part of your great-grandparents' lives. Look for clues in the settings described below. Before each setting, write *past, present,* or *can't tell*.

_____ 1. David was going to be late to work again. During the night the power had gone off, and his radio alarm did not go off at the usual time.

_____ 2. The army lieutenant rode across the vast prairie. For three days he had not seen a single human being. He figured he had two days more to ride before reaching Fort Roundhill. There a letter might be waiting for him. That is, if the Pony Express was still carrying mail.

_____ 3. It was a great event: The transcontinental railroad was finally completed. Now passengers could board the train in New York City and travel across the entire United States. Would wonders never cease!

_____ 4. The Baldwin family boarded their plane in Boston at midnight. It was 7:00 A.M. in London. They would be having dinner in London the next evening. It made Anne's head swim to think that they would cross the Atlantic Ocean before breakfast.

_____ 5. Charles Lindbergh could hardly believe it when his small plane touched down outside Paris, France. Crowds of people were standing there, cheering. News of his approach had reached Paris by telegraph. He was the first man to cross the Atlantic Ocean by plane!

_____ 6. Jane sat reading by the window. Outside she could see the gardeners raking leaves. It wouldn't be long before the trees were bare and the garden paths were covered in snow. She and her brothers would build a snowman on the lawn. She wondered where her boots and mittens were.

_____ 7. Waves of people with umbrellas poured across the slippery street. On a night like this, nothing was harder to find in New York City than an empty cab! Albert was surprised when a smart-looking carriage drove up. His friend Damien leaned out the window and called, "Can I give you a lift home?"

_____ 8. Marilyn studied hard and made good grades. Her friend June thought she should be having more fun. "Don't you have time for a movie this weekend?" she asked. "I have to keep my grades up," Marilyn told her friend. "You know how hard it is to get into the astronaut program."

Teaching the Short Story Curriculum Guide © 1994 Lake Education, Belmont CA

SETTING: Settings in Your Life

Name _____ Date _____

Not every story is set in a faraway place or a time in the past. If you were to write a story about your own life, you would use settings that you know well. Answer the following questions to get started on describing the settings in your life.

1. What is the name of your city, town, or community?

    _____

2. What three words would you use to describe what you like best about your

    city or town? _____

3. What three words would you use to describe what you like *least* about it?

    _____

4. What three words would you use to describe the look and feel of your

    house or apartment? _____

5. What kind of music can be heard in your house? _____

6. How many people live with you? _____ Who are they? _____

    _____

7. Is your house a quiet place or a noisy place? _____

    What kind of sounds do you hear there? _____

    _____

8. Where do you like to go to relax? _____

    Describe that place. _____

    _____

9. What is your favorite time of year? _____

    What do you like about it? _____

    _____

10. What three words describe your school or workplace? _____

    _____

11. If you could live any place you wanted, where would that be? Explain why

    that place seems so attractive to you. _____

    _____

    _____

    _____

SETTING: Writing About Setting, Advanced

Name _____ Date _____

Choose at least three of the four places suggested below. Write four sentences to describe each place. Imagine that you are writing for someone who has never seen this place before.

1. **My Bedroom** (how big it is, what you can see from the window, what special things are in it)

   _____

   _____

   _____

   _____

   _____

2. **Outside My Front Door** (what you can see, what you can hear, what you like to see, what you don't like to see)

   _____

   _____

   _____

   _____

   _____

3. **Where I Am Right Now** (what you can see, hear, feel; what is special, ordinary, what is going on)

   _____

   _____

   _____

   _____

   _____

4. **A Place I Dreamed About** (where it was, how things looked, how it made you feel, who was there)

   _____

   _____

   _____

   _____

   _____

SETTING: Story Report

Name _____ Date _____

---

1. Name of story _____

2. Author _____ Born _____ Died _____

3. What is the setting of the story (city, country, kind of building, etc.)?

   _____

   _____

4. About when does the story take place (year, season, time of day, etc.)?

   _____

5. What clues in the story help you to place it in time (clothing, transportation, conversation, objects, words, way of life, etc.)?

   _____

   _____

   _____

6. Write three sentences from the story that describe the setting.

   _____

   _____

   _____

7. How important is the setting to the story? For example, would the story be the same if it happened at another place? In another time? Explain your answer.

   _____

   _____

   _____

8. Imagine that you are in the place where the story is set. Name three things that you would see, feel, or hear there. Write a sentence of your own that describes each thing.

   _____   _____

                                 _____

   _____   _____

                                 _____

   _____   _____

                                 _____

PLOT: Defining Plot

Name _____ Date _____

Look up the term *plot* in your glossary. Write the definition here.

_____

_____

Now think about plot as you read the following paragraphs. Then answer the questions below.

a.   Only 50 years ago, there were large herds of wild horses living in the western United States. By now, most of them have been captured. Some went to new homes on ranches, but many were killed. The story of our wild horses is a sad one.

b.   We had never seen so many wild geese before. Their honking filled the air. Hundreds were already on the lake and hundreds more were landing. The sky was dark with birds. It was a thrilling sight.

c.   The boys were mountain-climbing when they discovered the wild fawn. They saw the mother doe a few yards away. She had been shot. The boys carried the fawn home and raised it on their farm. The next year they released the young doe in the mountains.

1.   Which paragraph above *does not* have an outcome?
     (Hint: There is no problem to be solved.) Paragraph _____

2.   In paragraph c, what problem has to be solved? _____

     _____

     _____

3.   In paragraph a, is the problem clearly stated? _____

     What do you think the problem might have been? _____

     _____

4.   In paragraph c, what is the outcome of the plot? (Hint: How is the

     problem solved?)_____

     _____

5.   In your opinion, which paragraph has the best story plot? _____

     Explain your answer. _____

     _____

PLOT: Analyzing Plot

Name _____ Date _____

1. **Look up the term *climax* in your glossary. Write the definition here.**

    _____

    _____

In each paragraph below, underline the sentence that states the climax. Beneath each paragraph, state the problem.

2. Every time the lieutenant looked back, he saw the wolf. When the lieutenant speeded up, so did the wolf. When he slowed down, so did the wolf. It seemed that the animal meant no harm, but the lieutenant felt uncomfortable riding with a wolf on his tail. After 20 minutes of dodging and wheeling on his horse, he gave up. If a wolf wanted to go along with him on his morning rides, so be it.

    State the problem: _____

    _____

3. Helen was born deaf and blind. Because she could not communicate with people, she was growing up like a wild creature. A teacher was found who could work with the deaf. This gifted woman taught Helen to communicate—first by touch and then with speech. Helen became a great communicator. Her example has inspired the world for decades.

    State the problem: _____

    _____

4. Gary did not want his mother to marry Maryann's dad. Maryann didn't want her father to marry Gary's mother. Neither child wanted to share his or her parent with the other child. But the parents got married anyway. "You kids will have to learn to be friends," they said. "We're not going to take sides." At the same moment, Gary and Maryann saw each other make a face. Then they both began to laugh. Perhaps it would be best if they became friends after all.

    State the problem: _____

    _____

5. Today was Harlan's birthday. Louise was taking him out to dinner tonight. But he was busy in the auto shop until an hour after closing. Harlan was covered with grease and grime. He knew he was running late when he screeched to a halt at his house. Making fast plans, he raced inside. "I can shower in ten minutes. I hope there's some shampoo. I have to shine my shoes too." "Surprise!" everybody yelled, as he bolted through the front door.

    State the problem: _____

    _____

PLOT: Story Structure, page 1

Name _____ Date _____

Read the story in the box. Think about *plot* as you read. Then answer the questions.

Alex asked his younger brother Ben to do him a big favor. "After school tomorrow, please go to my studio. Wrap up the big painting on the easel. Take it to the museum and enter it in the mixed media show for me. I have to be at work all day."

Ben had taken paintings to the museum for Alex before. He knew what to do. Today, he did just as Alex had asked. Except for one thing. He knocked over a bucket of shellac in the studio and dropped the painting in it!

Ben knew the shellac was transparent. Maybe it wouldn't show. He wrapped the painting in brown paper and took it to the museum. Once there he unwrapped the painting and put it in the jury room to be judged. Ben was horrified to see that the brown paper stuck to the painting in big patches! Then the judges came into the room. Ben panicked and ran.

When Ben finally fell asleep that night, he had terrible dreams. All night he tossed and turned. At school the next day, he went through his classes like a zombie. There was a knot in his stomach, and his head hurt. But he had an idea. He would go straight to the museum after school. Perhaps someone there could help him fix the wrecked painting. If not, then he would just have to tell his brother. The thought made his headache worse.

After school, Ben raced to the museum and headed into the jury room. Alex's painting was not there. His heart began to pound. Panicked, Ben ran into the main gallery. What he saw stopped him cold.

Alex's painting hung right by the door. Beside it was a neatly lettered card that said, *Fragments, by Alex Johnson.* Above that hung another card that said, "First Place."

The brown paper and shellac looked just great on the piles of thick paint. The painting was a knockout.

---

1. Name the two characters in the story. _____

2. Choose the best summary of the story's plot. Circle the letter of your answer.

   a. Thinking he has wrecked his brother's painting, Ben spends a sleepless night. To his surprise, the painting wins first place.

   b. Upsetting a bucket of shellac, Ben wrecks his brother's painting. He is afraid to tell his brother what happened.

   c. Ben wrecks his brother's painting. What if the judges find out?

3. What is the climax of the story? _____

   _____

4. Write a title for the story. _____

PLOT: Story Structure, page 2

Name _____ Date _____

All the action in a story builds to the *climax,* or outcome. You can see
this clearly if you break the story into parts, or scenes. Imagine that the
story you just read is the plot for a TV episode. The show is a comedy
called *Alex and Ben.* The setting is a big city. The characters are Alex
Johnson, the artist, and his younger brother Ben. The scenes are listed
in order below. Write what happens in each scene.

1. Morning, at home: _____
    _____

2. Afternoon, Alex's studio: _____
    _____

3. Afternoon, museum jury room: _____
    _____

4. Night, at home: _____
    _____

5. The next day, at school: _____
    _____

6. That afternoon, museum jury room: _____
    _____

7. Museum main gallery: _____
    _____

8. In which scene is the main problem stated? _____

9. What is the problem? _____
    _____

10. In which scene does the climax of the story take place? _____

11. Which character is the main actor in all these scenes? _____

12. In which scene or scenes do you think Ben is the most upset? _____

13. The story could have a final scene, one that takes place after the climax.

    Write a final scene for the story. _____
    _____
    _____
    _____

PLOT: Plots in Your Life, Advanced

Name _____ Date _____

People's lives are filled with plots. Everyone has problems to solve, conflicts, and resolutions. Some outcomes make you happy, some outcomes make you sad, and other outcomes just lead to more problems to solve.

There is at least one plot in the story of your life today. It may not be very exciting, but it contains a problem that needs a resolution. Fill in the blanks to get a clearer picture of the plots in your life.

1. List six of the most important things that you did today. List them in the order in which you did them.

    _____

    _____

    _____

    _____

    _____

    _____

    Does each of the things you did lead to the next thing? If so, you have the beginning structure for a plot. If one thing does not lead to the next thing, you may revise the events to make this happen. (You can even make up an event or two.)

2. Describe one problem you had today. _____

    _____

3. How did you resolve the problem? (Or how did the problem solve itself?)

    _____

    _____

4. Now you have the elements of a plot. Write these elements below.

    characters _____

    setting _____

    problem or conflict _____

    _____

    resolution (or non-resolution) _____

    _____

    conclusion _____

    _____

PLOT: Writing About Plot

Name _____ Date _____

Read the four problems described below. Now build a story plot around one of the problems. Fill in the blanks on the Plot Outline.

a. A group of Vietnam veterans want to build a memorial in their state. But there are no state funds for such a project.

b. Dave Gibbons is worried about his son, Robert. The boy is getting bad grades and skipping school. Dave wants Robert's behavior to change.

c. Derrick Morris wants to fight crime in his neighborhood. He has no idea where he should begin.

d. For 10 years, Alice Morgan has worked as a clerk at City Hospital. Now she's been laid off along with many others. She wants to train for a different kind of job.

Plot Outline

TOPIC _____

CHARACTERS _____

SETTING _____

_____

PROBLEM _____

_____

EVENTS THAT LEAD TO RESOLUTION

1. _____

2. _____

3. _____

4. _____

5. _____

STORY OUTCOME _____

_____

_____

_____

Teaching the Short Story Curriculum Guide © 1994 Lake Education, Belmont CA

PLOT: Story Report, page 1

Name _____ Date _____

Story title _____

Author _____ Born _____ Died _____

1. Who are the main characters in the story? Write a sentence to describe
   each one. _____

   _____

2. What is the setting and time of the story? _____

   _____

3. Write a brief summary of the story. Be sure to mention all the main
   events. _____

   _____

   _____

   _____

   _____

   _____

   _____

4. What is the main conflict or problem in the story? _____

   _____

   _____

   _____

5. Is the conflict *internal* (a character's struggle with himself or herself) or
   external (with other characters or forces)? Perhaps it is both internal *and*
   external. Explain your answer. _____

   _____

   _____

   _____

6. Find the sentence or sentences in the story that state the climax. Write
   those sentences here. _____

   _____

   _____

   _____

PLOT: Story Report, page 2

Name _____ Date _____

7. Does anything happen after the climax? _____ Does the author provide
   a conclusion? What is it? _____
   _____
   _____

8. Is the end of the story surprising? _____ Why or why not? _____
   _____
   _____

9. Is the focus of the story mostly on *character, plot,* or *setting?* Explain your
   answer. _____
   _____
   _____

10. Did the author build suspense in the story? If so, how? _____
    _____
    _____

11. What did you think was the most interesting part of the story? Why did
    you think so? _____
    _____
    _____

12. How do the main characters feel about the outcome of the story? Does the
    author let you know? If not, what is your opinion? _____
    _____
    _____

13. Think of a different way to end the story. Write your new ending here.
    _____
    _____
    _____
    _____
    _____

CHARACTER: Defining Character

Name _____ Date _____

1. **Look up the term *character* in your glossary. Write the definition here.**

   _____

   _____

2. The characters in a story are the actors who take part in the story. Because story characters are imaginary, we call them "literary characters." Sometimes you may hear someone speak of another person as a "real character." That usually means that this person has some unusual qualities.

   The word *character* has a number of meanings. Which sentence below uses "character" to mean "person from a story"? Circle a letter to show your answer.

   a. I sat next to some character on the bus who told me he was Napoleon.

   b. Martin Luther King was a man of strong character.

   c. The Rocky Mountains are different in character from the Alleghenies.

   d. Martin likes to play character roles.

   e. My favorite character in *The Three Musketeers* is d'Artagnan.

3. We meet literary characters all the time in books, movies, TV, plays, and musical productions. Movie actors sometimes become famous for playing a famous character. Some such well-known characters are Sherlock Holmes, James Bond's Agent 007, or Shakespeare's Hamlet.

   As children we meet literary characters in nursery rhymes, fairy tales, comic books, and other stories. Which of the characters listed below have you met? Circle the names of those you know.

Cinderella	Superman	Peter Rabbit
Snow White	Robin Hood	Pogo
Peter Pan	Aladdin	Mary Poppins
Robinson Crusoe	Wonder Woman	Winnie the Pooh

4. Choose one of the characters from the above list. Write three or four sentences about him or her. Include a phyical description, the character's age, and something that makes the character special. Write on the back of this sheet if you need more room.

   _____

   _____

   _____

CHARACTER: Analyzing Character

Name _____ Date _____

Character is one of the most powerful of the literary elements. Long after you have forgotten the plot and setting of a story, you may remember a striking character. This is because we are interested in what other human beings do, think, and say.

1. In bringing a story character to life, an author uses description, dialogue (both speech and thoughts), and narration. Label the four sentences as *description*, *dialogue*, or *narration*. (Use your glossary if you need help.)

   a. George was tall, but not as tall as he wanted to be. At sixteen, he was still a head shorter than his father. _____

   b. "No!" George shouted. "You can't tell me what to do! I won't give up football!" _____

   c. "Yikes," Angie thought. "That girl can really skate. If my jumps aren't higher than hers, she'll beat me." _____

   d. Angie took time to inspect her skates. She remembered what her coach had told her about relaxing. She smiled and began her routine.

   _____

2. The sentences above give you certain facts about the characters. Circle the letters of the following sentences that give facts.

   a. George is tall.   b. George is six feet tall.

   c. George wants to be as tall as his father.   d. George likes football.

   e. Angie is a skater.   f. Angie is afraid.

   g. Angie can jump.   h. Angie is competing.

3. What other guesses can you make about George and Annie. Find four good guesses below. Circle a letter to show each answer.

   i. George has a temper.   j. George is angry with his father.

   k. George has a conflict.   l. George will give up football.

   m. Angie is careful   n. Angie listens to her coach.

   o. Angie will win.   p. Angie wants to win.

4. Invent some more information about George or Angie. You may use description, dialogue, or narration. Write three or four sentences about the character on the back of this sheet. (The facts should fit what you already know).

Teaching the Short Story Curriculum Guide © 1994 Lake Education, Belmont CA

CHARACTER: Understanding Characters

Name _____ Date _____

As a story develops, we learn what the characters are like. We find out what they think and feel, and how they behave. A skillful writer creates characters that seem real. As we get to know them, we can often predict what they will do. In a story, different characters respond differently to the same situation—just as people do in real life.

Read the two paragraphs below. Then answer the questions.

Walking among the great, tall trees, Marty felt awe. He loved to see the sturdy, silent giants, rising high into the sky. The forest gave him a sense of peace and comfort. Suddenly Marty knew that he wanted to stay here. He felt a great hunger to discover all there was to know about life in this ancient forest. There seemed no end to what he could learn here.

As Howard walked among the great, tall trees, he heard faint scurrying sounds. The leaves and twigs under his feet seemed to make explosive snaps. What unknown things might be lurking behind these dark shadows? Very little light filtered through the treetops. The old forest seemed filled with danger and gloom. A deep sense of loneliness came over Howard. How he longed for bright lights and the familiar sounds of people laughing and talking!

1. The setting of both paragraphs is an ancient forest. Do Marty and Howard feel the same way about the setting? _____

2. Which character feels that the forest is a good place to be? _____

3. What word might describe how the other character feels about the forest?

    _____

4. The writer's words show us the forest through the eyes of each character. Which character sees the trees as "sturdy, silent giants"? _____

5. The other character sees the forest as filled with _____ and

    _____.

6. Based on their reactions to the forest, we can see that Marty and Howard are very different. Which character is more likely to enjoy spending time alone? _____ Does the writer tell us in so many words? _____

7. Which character probably prefers to live in a city? _____ How does the writer suggest that? _____

    _____

CHARACTER: Characters in Your Life

Name _____ Date _____

Story characters do not pop up out of nowhere. Writers create characters from what they know about other people, about themselves, and about life. That is one of the reasons that every writer's work is unique.

Your life is filled with characters. Each character probably belongs to many different categories. For example, if your father is a policeman, he belongs to two categories: policeman and father. He belongs to many other categories as well, such as friend, son, husband.

First, list the names of three people you know. Then list two categories to which each person belongs.

	PERSON	CATEGORY 1	CATEGORY 2
1.	_____	_____	_____
2.	_____	_____	_____
3.	_____	_____	_____

Now choose one person from your list. Write two sentences describing that person's physical qualities (age, height, coloring, etc.).

4. _____

5. _____

Write two sentences describing the person's occupation. (child, student, waiter, etc.)

6. _____

7. _____

Write two sentences describing the person's likes and dislikes.

8. _____

9. _____

Write the two most interesting facts about the person.

10. _____

11. _____

Write a sentence telling how the two of you are different. Write another telling how you are alike.

12. _____

13. _____

CHARACTER: Writing About Characters, Advanced

Name _____ Date _____

Choose one or more of the assignments below. Then write on the lines below. If you need more room, write on the back of this sheet.

1. **Write about your best friend.** Give the person's age, name, and some physical characteristics. Name some likes and dislikes. Describe something you like to do together. Explain why you like him or her. Write one line of dialogue that sounds like something he or she would say.

2. **Write about an astronuat, real or imaginary.** Give his or her age and some physical characteristics. Name some things you think he or she would like or dislike; describe some goals the astronaut might have and how he or she might have reached them. Describe one possible conflict. Write a line of dialogue that sounds like something he or she might say.

3. **Write about yourself.** Give your name, age, sex, and some physical characteristics. Describe the way you see yourself. Imagine some ways that others might see you. Tell about some of your likes and dislikes, your goals and fears. Describe your family. Describe one conflict. Write a line of dialogue that sounds like you.

4. **Invent a character.** Tell what he or she looks like, where he or she lives, and what he or she does. Describe likes and dislikes, goals and fears. Tell about a conflict. What do you find interesting about this character? Explain your thinking.

5. **Choose a famous person or a character from history.** Read about him or her in the library. Write a paragraph about this person, using the instructions for the paragraphs above. Explain why this person interests you.

My Paragraph Title _____

_____

_____

_____

_____

_____

_____

_____

_____

_____

_____

CHARACTER: Story Report

Name _____ Date _____

Story Title _____

Author _____ Born _____ Died _____

Name three characters from the story. Write one fact about each.

1. _____ _____

2. _____ _____

3. _____ _____

4. Who is the main character in the story? _____

5. Write three sentences describing the main character.

   _____

   _____

   _____

6. Describe the conflict or problem the main character faces.

   _____

   _____

7. How is this conflict or problem resolved?

   _____

   _____

8. Does the story outcome make the main character happy? Explain.

   _____

   _____

9. What are your feelings about the main character?

   _____

   _____

10. Write three lines of dialogue from the story that help the reader
    understand the main character.

   _____

   _____

   _____

THEME: Defining Theme

Name _____ Date _____

Look up the term *theme* in your glossary. Write the definition here.

_____

_____

Every story has a theme. Some of the major literary themes are listed below. Write a statement that you believe to be true about each theme.

1. love _____

2. courage _____

3. honor _____

4. poverty _____

5. change _____

6. family _____

7. death _____

8. justice _____

9. war _____

10. time _____

11. art _____

12. happiness _____

Authors usually want to deliver a message about their themes. This message is often a statement of belief. The story expresses this message. The sentences you wrote above are thematic statements. Choose one of your thematic statements and write a paragraph explaining it. Use the back of this sheet if you need more room.

_____

_____

_____

_____

_____

_____

THEME: Analyzing Theme

Name _____ Date _____

Read the list of literary themes.

love	disappointment	courage	injustice
honor	war	kindness	art
family	happiness	sacrifice	ambition
hope	misunderstanding	greed	revenge

Part I   Plot and Theme: Decide what theme might be expressed by each of the story plots below. (Some plots may express more than one theme.)

1. A boy tries to impress his girlfriend, but he makes a fool of himself instead. _____

2. A soldier risks his life in battle to save the life of a friend. _____

3. After long years of study and practice, Amy wins a major piano competition. _____

4. A famous lawyer finds true happiness by giving up his career to become a painter. _____

5. A mother gives up a chance to star in a movie in order to be with her children. _____

6. A father takes his daughters on a special outing. _____

7. A child protects a wild animal from a greedy hunter. _____

Part II   Thematic Statements: Decide what theme is expressed by each of the statements below. You may use the themes listed above.

8. Time helps people get over losses. _____

9. Teenagers often have difficulty getting along with their families. _____

10. Harrison discovered that his vast fortune brought him no happiness. _____

11. It is wrong for strong people to take advantage of the weak. _____

12. There is almost always a chance that a bad situation can improve. _____

THEME: Writing About Theme, Advanced

Name _____ Date _____

Think about the themes listed below. Write a story plot in one or two sentences for each theme.

1. courage _____
   _____
   _____

2. success _____
   _____
   _____

3. revenge _____
   _____
   _____

4. hard work _____
   _____
   _____

5. justice _____
   _____
   _____

6. ambition _____
   _____
   _____

7. love _____
   _____
   _____

8. change _____
   _____
   _____

9. family _____
   _____
   _____

Teaching the Short Story Curriculum Guide © 1994 Lake Education, Belmont CA

THEME: Story Report

Name _____ Date _____

Choose three stories that you have read. Analyze their themes on the lines below. Read the example before you begin.

Title *The Return of a Private*   Author *Hamlin Garland*

Story Theme (one or two words) *war; family*

Story Theme Statement (one or two sentences) *War is cruel. But love can heal.*

Explain how the story illustrates its theme. *Private Smith returns home from the Civil War, sick and worried about the future. His young wife and children are so happy to have him home that his faith in life is restored.*

1. Title_____ Author_____

   Story Theme_____

   Story Theme Statement _____

   _____

   Explain how the story illustrates its theme. _____

   _____

   _____

2. Title_____ Author_____

   Story Theme_____

   Story Theme Statement _____

   _____

   Explain how the story illustrates its theme. _____

   _____

   _____

3. Title_____ Author_____

   Story Theme_____

   Story Theme Statement _____

   _____

   Explain how the story illustrates its theme. _____

   _____

   _____

TONE AND MOOD: Defining Tone, page 1

Name _____ Date _____

1. **Look up the word *tone* in your glossary. Write the definition here.**

   _____

   _____

Authors use a wide variety of tones. Decide what tone the author is using in each paragraph below. Choose a term from the box to label each paragraph. (You may want to use more than one term.)

suspicious	humorous	mysterious
hopeless	sarcastic	confiding
frightening	pestering	formal

2. How this book came to be written, nobody knows. Nobody but me, that is— and it took me a long time to decide to tell the strange story. At one time this story could have been dangerous for little Billy and his dad. But now that they're gone, it doesn't matter.

   _____

3. James Tarlow was six feet tall when he was ten, and some folks say he was five feet long at birth. Everybody in that family was so tall, they just plain took all the ceilings out of their house. The Tarlows had dogs the size of ponies. Nobody ever knew what they did for beds. Maybe they slept with their feet sticking out of the windows.

   _____

4. You wouldn't believe what a rowdy family the Craigs are! It is nothing to see them rolling around on the floor or shouting at the top of their lungs. I'm afraid to take a drink in their house. I shouldn't spread this around, but one time my water glass had a fish in it! Don't tell anyone what I said about the Craigs.

   _____

TONE AND MOOD: Defining Tone, page 2

Name _____ Date _____

5. The detective lifted his eyebrows as he listened to Barney's story. Now and then a small smile tugged at the corners of his mouth. Barney's alibi certainly showed a lot of imagination. But the detective couldn't quite believe that the diamond ring fell into Barney's pocket by accident.

_____

6. Kerry hadn't seen her dad in three years. After his divorce from her mother, he had moved to Hawaii and gotten married again. At first he had written to Kerry once in a while and he called a few times. But now she hadn't heard from him in more than a year. She took his picture off of her nightstand and put it in a bottom drawer.

_____

7. Shana's apology was *very* convincing—if you believe that pigs can fly! You could tell how sincere she was by the smirk on her face. I was especailly touched when she rolled her eyes at her friends who were standing behind me. I'm sure she would have said she was sorry even if the principal hadn't made her do it. *Sure*!

_____

8. I knew that the howling would begin again at the stroke of midnight. The same thing had been happening every night for weeks. And every night the terrible sound got louder. I knew that the beast was closing in. What I didn't know was why it had chosen me as its victim. No one else could hear the howling at all.

_____

TONE AND MOOD: Defining Mood

Name _____ Date _____

Look up the term *mood* in your glossary. Write the definition here.

_____

_____

You have seen how authors use different tones in their writing. In the same way, an author uses language to create a variety of moods.

Read the following passage from Washington Irving's story, *The Devil and Tom Walker*. Think about *mood* as you read.

> One day Tom Walker had been to a distant part of the neighborhood. He took what he thought was a short cut home. The way led him through the swamp. Like most short cuts, it was a poorly chosen path. The swamp was thickly grown with gloomy trees, some of them ninety feet high. Though it was noon, it was very dark. Pits and quicksand were partly covered with green weeds and mosses. This often tricked travelers into stepping into the black, smothering mud. There were dark, silent pools where lived the bull-frog and the water-snake. Trunks of trees lay half drowned, half rotting. They looked like alligators sleeping in the mud.

1. Which word best describes the mood of the passage? Circle the word.

    romantic   playful   gloomy   inspiring

2. On the lines below, copy six words or phrases from the passage that help to create the mood.

    _____   _____

    _____   _____

    _____   _____

3. The passage prepares the reader for the next thing that will happen in the story. What kind of story event do you think this will be? Circle the word.

    wonderful   scary   foolish   funny

4. The character in the passage must have some feelings about his surroundings. Circle the word that probably describes Tom Walker's mood.

    calm   fearful   joyful   suspicious

TONE AND MOOD: Analyzing Mood

Name _____ Date _____

Decide what mood each paragraph expresses. Write a term from the box after each paragraph.

excitement	sadness	loneliness
joy	despair	fear

1. Frank gazed at the still features of his gradmother's face. He saw a lifetime of sacrifice etched in the many lines. She looked peaceful in death. But Frank's heart ached to think that he would never hear her voice again.

   _____

2. The arriving sailors poured off the ship, into the arms of waiting loved ones. Bands played along the dock. Babies nestled in fathers' arms. Toddlers rode high above the crowd on their fathers' shoulders. Tears of happiness streamed down many a face, and no one was ashamed.

   _____

3. Would tomorrow never come! Angela tossed and turned. Her bags were packed and waiting by the door. Her new outfit hung at the end of the bed. A new life would begin tomorrow, in far-away Africa! Every thought she had of morning drove sleep even farther from her grasp.

   _____

4. The wind whistled forlornly through the canyon. An eagle floated high above. It was the only living thing in John's sight. His companions had left yesterday morning. Now he felt like the only person left alive on the face of the earth. He spoke loudly to his shadow. Anything to hear the sound of a human voice!

   _____

5. The tornado had taken everything. *Everything*! The little family huddled together, gazing at the wreckage of their farm. Not a post was left standing. Not a stalk of corn remained in the fields. Robert thought of his long hours of labor in the heat and the cold. He covered his face with his hands and wept soundlessly.

   _____

6. In three minutes the bomb would go off. Gus felt cold chills as he heard the bomb ticking. He struggled with the rope that tied his hands behind his back. Unless he could disarm the bomb, he was a dead man.

   _____

TONE AND MOOD: Writing About Mood, Advanced

Name _____ Date _____

The special effects in a movie are often used to create an intense mood. Authors use language to make special effects. Their artful language creates a mood in their stories.

Part I **Rewrite the following three sentences to create a *mysterious* mood.**

1. The door opened. _____
   _____

2. It was night. _____
   _____

3. The house was very old. _____
   _____

Rewrite the next three sentences to express a *joyful* mood.

4. Mom's birthday is tomorrow. _____
   _____

5. They got married. _____
   _____

6. He won the race. _____
   _____

Part II **Now write two short paragraphs that express mood. Choose two subjects from this list or use subjects of your own: *a tornado, a fight, a baby's birth, a stolen purse, a lost job, a graduation, an illness*. Write on the back of this sheet if you need more room.**

_____
_____
_____
_____
_____
_____
_____

TONE AND MOOD: Story Report

Name _____ Date _____

Think about the stories you have read. Choose a story that has an especially strong mood. Find examples in the story of words the author used to create that mood. As you read, copy down the words and the page numbers. Use the form below to write your story report about mood.

Before you begin, read the sample story report in the box.

Title: *The Pomegranate Seed*   Author: *Edith Wharton*

Mood of story: *Mysterious*

Words the author uses to create mood: *uneasiness (p.17) dangerous bomb (p.25) secret (p.22) suffering, dread (p.32) mysterious (p.33) invisible (p.34) worry (p.37) fear and hatred, dismay and anger (p.46) ghost (p.47)*

Sentences that create mood: *Her mother-in-law leaned against the table. Her voice was sad. "But we're going mad. We're both going mad. Both of us know that such things are impossible." (p.46)*

Charlotte laughed again. "I suppose everything's pale about a ghost," she said. (p.47)

Charlotte cut her short. "An explanation? Who's going to give it, I wonder?" (p.48)

Title: _____   Author: _____

Mood of story: _____

Words the author uses to create mood: _____

_____

_____

Sentences that create mood: _____

_____

_____

_____

_____

_____

_____

Glossary

action what happens in a story; the acts or events that take place

> The adventure story about mountain-climbing is full of action.

art the human activity of creating things that have form and beauty

> She is interested in science, and he is interested in art.

art form a branch of the arts such as literature, music, painting, or dance

> Rug-weaving is a Native American art form.

author the writer of a book or article, etc.

> Stephen King is a famous American author.

author's purpose the author's specific goal or reason for writing a certain story or book

> The author's purpose in writing the story was to make fun of power-mad politicians.

character a fictional person who plays a part in a story

> Superman is a popular comic book character.

climax the outcome of the story's main conflict

> The rescue of the drowning men was the story's climax.

conflict the struggle between forces at the center of the story; the conflict may be within a character, between characters, or between characters and an outside force, such as war

> The story's conflict was resolved when Reggie won the race.

effect in literature, an impression created by the writer

> Poe's horror stories often create a gloomy effect.

event a specific occurrence; something that happens

> The theft of the ring was the first event in the detective story.

description the parts of a story or book that tell about the appearance of the setting or characters

> Her detailed description of the old house made us feel that we were there.

dialogue words spoken by the characters in a story or play

> The dialogue between the competing athletes was very realistic.

fiction a literary work in which the plot and characters are the products of the author's imagination

> *Huckleberry Finn* is a fine example of American fiction.

foreshadowing hints an author places in a story of events that will happen later

> The death of his pet foreshadowed the end of the boy's childhood.

imagery figures of speech that help the reader to visualize the characters or setting

> The author used imagery when he described the thief as "hatchet-faced."

introduction a short reading that presents and explains a story or book; sometimes the first part of a story or book that sets the scene

The introduction said that the story was set in the future.

irony a literary device; the gap, often humorous, between the real and the unreal; the opposite of what is expected

The irony was that the prison guard was soft-hearted.

literature the body of written work including all forms, such as fiction, non-fiction, poetry, drama, etc.

Every country has its own body of literature.

literary form a certain type of written work, such as the short story, the novel, the poem, etc.

The essay is a literary form.

mood the overall feeling or atmosphere the author creates in a story

The story about the circus had a joyful mood.

moral the instructive point of a story; the lesson to be drawn by the reader

The moral of the story was a warning about jealousy.

motive the driving force, either internal or external, that makes a character do something

The stranger seemed to be kindly, but his real motive was greed.

narrator, narration the character who tells the story in his or her own words; the telling of a story's events

A character named Ishmael is the narrator of _Moby Dick_.

non-fiction books or articles about real people or actual events

How to Sell Real Estate is a book of non-fiction.

novel a long form of fictional literature with a complex plot

Gone With the Wind has been a popular novel for 50 years.

novella a short novel

Most people can't read a whole novella in one sitting.

pace the speed at which a story develops and moves along

The exciting shipwreck story moves at a very fast pace.

passage a section of a written work; may be just one line or several paragraphs

His favorite passage from the book is on page 6.

plot the chain of events in a story that leads to its outcome

The plot of the mystery story had many surprising twists and turns.

point of view the mental position from which a character sees the events of the story unfold

Different characters may have very different points of view of the same event.

protagonist the main character in a story or book

Scarlett O'Hara is the protagonist of _Gone With the Wind_.

quotation the exact words spoken by a character; the words set off between quotation marks

"To be or not to be?" is a famous quotation from Shakespeare's _Hamlet_.

realism the author's emphasis on showing life as it really is, not romanticized or idealized

Chekhov wrote about the lives of Russian peasants with great realism.

resolution the conclusion of the story's conflict; the outcome of the struggle

The resolution of the story came about when the enemy retreated.

sequence the order in which story events happen

If you read the last page of a story first, you are reading out of sequence.

setting where and when a story takes place; the location and time

"An Occurrence at Owl Creek Bridge" is set in the South during the Civil War.

short story the fictional form that is shorter than the novel; usually focused on a single effect and having few characters

"The Big Blonde" is a famous short story by Ernest Hemingway.

structure the underlying form of a story; the way it is put together

Some stories are structured around the characters, and some are structured around the plot.

style the special way a writer uses language to express both literary form and his or her experience

O. Henry wrote many stories in a light-hearted, sentimental style.

suspense the sense of intense interest and excitement that builds before a story's outcome is revealed

"The Tell-Tale Heart" is a masterpiece of slowly building suspense.

symbol a person or thing that stands for, or represents, something else

The dove is a symbol for peace.

theme the central meaning of a story; the main idea; the point

Revenge is the theme of "The Cask of Amontillado."

tone the feeling given by the author's voice; the attitude expressed by the author's use of language

The tone of Hawthorne's stories is serious rather than playful.

turning point the high point of interest in a story; the place at which the outcome begins to unfold

The criminal's confession was the turning point of the story.

twist an unexpected turn of events in a story's plot

The discovery of buried treasure was a surprising twist in the plot.

voice the author's unique way of telling a story; a combination of personality and use of literary tools; the quality that sets one writer apart from other writers

Shakespeare's voice is unique in all of literature.

VOCABULARY EXERCISE

Name _____ Date _____

Look through the story and find at least ten words that are new to you. List the words on the lines below and then look them up in a dictionary. Finally, use each word in a sentence of your own.

Story title _____

1. _____   6. _____
2. _____   7. _____
3. _____   8. _____
4. _____   9. _____
5. _____   10. _____

1. _____
   _____
2. _____
   _____
3. _____
   _____
4. _____
   _____
5. _____
   _____
6. _____
   _____
7. _____
   _____
8. _____
   _____
9. _____
   _____
10. _____
   _____

Studying the Short Story

GENERIC STORY REPORT

Name _____ Date _____

Title of Story _____

Author _____

Three facts about the author

_____

_____

_____

Author's purpose in this story (examples: to entertain, frighten, instruct, inform, etc.):

_____

Setting: Place and time of the story _____

_____

Plot: What happens in the story? Write two or three sentences.

_____

_____

_____

_____

What is the conflict?

_____

_____

_____

Character: Name two or three of the main characters. Write a sentence about each one.

_____

_____

_____

_____

What did you like best about the story?

_____

_____

_____

_____

Teaching the Short Story Curriculum Guide © 1994 Lake Education, Belmont CA

GENERIC STORY REPORT, Advanced

Name _____ Date _____

---

1. Story title _____

   Author _____

   How does the title relate to the story? _____

   _____

   Is the story title interesting? Why or why not? _____

   _____

2. What type of story is it? Choose one or more of the following types: *adventure, love, detective, fantasy, war, horror, science fiction, slice of life,* or name a type of your own. Find a sentence from the story that supports your opinion. Write it on the line provided.

   Type of story _____

   Sentence from the story _____

   _____

   _____

3. What is the story's *theme* (the main idea the story illustrates)? Some thematic statements are: *Wealth does not guarantee happiness, crime doesn't pay, home is the best place to be,* and so on. After writing a thematic statement, copy a sentence from the story that supports your opinion.

   Thematic statement _____

   Sentence from the story _____

   _____

   _____

4. What was the most important *element* in this story—*setting, character,* or *plot?*

   Most important element _____

   Explain your opinion. _____

   _____

   _____

   Examples from the story that support your opinion. _____

   _____

   _____

   _____

TIME LINE: The United States

Name _____ Date _____

(1775) America's Revolutionary War begins

(1781) The British surrender at Yorktown

(1793) Invention of the cotton gin

(1800) Thomas Jefferson elected president

(1803) U.S. buys Louisiana Territory

(1820) First canning factory in the U.S.

(1830) American Indians forced west of the Mississippi

(1840) Pioneers travel the Oregon Trail

(1848) Gold discovered in California

(1861) Lincoln elected president; Civil War begins

(1865) Lincoln assassinated; Civil War ends

(1879) Edison invents the electric light

(1886) Statue of Liberty goes up in New York Harbor

(1898) Spanish-American War

(1904) New York subway opens

(1908) Ford invents the Model T 1910

(1914) Panana Canal opens

(1920) First regular radio broadcast in U.S.

(1927) Lindbergh makes solo flight over the Atlantic

(1929) Stock market crash; Great Depression begins

(1937) Jet engine invented

(1941– 1945) U.S. fights in World War II

1770	(	)	
1780	(	)	
1790	(	)	
1800	(	)	
1810	(	)	
1820	(	)	
1830	(	)	
1840	(	)	
1850	(	)	
1860	(	)	
1870	(	)	
1880	(	)	
1890	(	)	
1900	(	)	
1910	(	)	
1920	(	)	
1930	(	)	
1940	(	)	
1950	(	)	

Teaching the Short Story Curriculum Guide © 1994 Lake Education, Belmont CA

TIME LINE: The World

Name _____ Date _____

(1770) Industrial Revolution begins in England	**1770**	( ) _____
(1778) Captain Cook discovers Hawaii		( ) _____
(1789) French Revolution begins	**1780**	( ) _____
(1799) Rosetta stone found in Egypt	**1790**	( ) _____
(1804) Napoleon crowns himself emperor		( ) _____
(1815) Napoleon defeated at Waterloo	**1800**	( ) _____
(1815) Russia: Bolshoi Ballet established	**1810**	( ) _____
(1833) Slavery abolished in British Empire		( ) _____
(1845) Potato famine in Ireland	**1820**	( ) _____
(1854–1856) Europe: Crimean War begins	**1830**	( ) _____
(1864) China: Taiping Rebellion ends after 13 years	**1840**	( ) _____
(1864) France: Louis Pasteur develops pasteurization	**1850**	( ) _____
(1867) Sweden: Alfred Nobel patents dynamite	**1860**	( ) _____
(1870–1871) Franco-Prussian War	**1870**	( ) _____
(1884) European countries scramble for colonies in Africa	**1880**	( ) _____
(1898) Cuba gains independence	**1890**	( ) _____
(1900) China: Boxer Rebellion; Hawaii becomes a state	**1900**	( ) _____
(1914) World War I declared in Europe	**1910**	( ) _____
(1917) Revolution in Russia		( ) _____
(1918) Allies win World War I	**1920**	( ) _____
(1927) Mussolini takes power in Italy		( ) _____
(1933) Hitler takes control of Germany	**1930**	( ) _____
(1939) Hitler invades Poland, World War II begins	**1940**	( ) _____
(1945) World War II ends	**1950**	( ) _____

STUDENT RECORD SHEET: Stories

Name _____ Date _____

	Story Title	Author	Date Read
1.	_____	_____	_____
2.	_____	_____	_____
3.	_____	_____	_____
4.	_____	_____	_____
5.	_____	_____	_____
6.	_____	_____	_____
7.	_____	_____	_____
8.	_____	_____	_____
9.	_____	_____	_____
10.	_____	_____	_____
11.	_____	_____	_____
12.	_____	_____	_____
13.	_____	_____	_____
14.	_____	_____	_____
15.	_____	_____	_____
16.	_____	_____	_____
17.	_____	_____	_____
18.	_____	_____	_____
19.	_____	_____	_____
20.	_____	_____	_____
21.	_____	_____	_____
22.	_____	_____	_____
23.	_____	_____	_____
24.	_____	_____	_____
25.	_____	_____	_____
26.	_____	_____	_____
27.	_____	_____	_____
28.	_____	_____	_____
29.	_____	_____	_____
30.	_____	_____	_____

Teaching the Short Story Curriculum Guide © 1994 Lake Education, Belmont CA

STUDENT RECORD SHEET: Exercises

Name _____ Date _____

Teaching the Short Story Curriculum Guide © 1994 Lake Education, Belmont CA

Date completed

Section I: The Art of Fiction

_____ 1   Categories of Art

_____ 2   The Writer's Tools

_____ 3   Story Elements

_____ 4   The Form of the Short Story

_____ 5   Types of Stories

_____ 6   Artful Language

_____ 7   Artful Language, Advanced

Section II: Setting

_____ 8   Defining Setting

_____ 9   Analyzing Setting

_____ 10   Setting and Time

_____ 11   Settings in Your Life

_____ 12   Writing About Setting, Advanced

_____ 13   Story Report: Setting

Section III: Plot

_____ 14   Defining Plot

_____ 15   Analyzing Plot

_____ 16   Story Structure (2 pages)

_____ 17   Plots in Your Life, Advanced

_____ 18   Writing About Plot

_____ 19   Story Report: Plot (2 pages)

Date completed

Section IV: Character

_____ 20   Defining Character

_____ 21   Analyzing Character

_____ 22   Understanding Characters

_____ 23   Characters in Your Life

_____ 24   Writing About Characters, Advanced

_____ 25   Story Report: Character

Section V: Theme

_____ 26   Defining Theme

_____ 27   Analyzing Theme

_____ 28   Writing About Theme, Advanced

_____ 29   Story Report: Theme

Section VI: Tone and Mood

_____ 30   Defining Tone (2 pages)

_____ 31   Defining Mood

_____ 32   Analyzing Mood

_____ 33   Writing About Mood, Advanced

_____ 34   Story Report: Tone and Mood